Permaculture for Beginners

Knowledge and Basics of Permaculture

©2019, Friedhelm Weiss

Published by Expertengruppe Verlag

Permaculture for Beginners

Knowledge and Basics of Permaculture

Published by Expertengruppe Verlag

TABLE OF CONTENTS

ABOUT THE AUTHOR

Friedhelm Weiss lives together with his wife Agatha and several animals in an old farmhouse in beautiful Rhineland.

For more than 50 years, he has oriented his life around the principles of permaculture. He has been working for many years on adjusting his own environment, particularly his house and land, to conform with the philosophy of permaculture.

Today, Friedhelm Weiss lives completely self-sufficiently and in harmony with the nature around him. He has reduced his footprint as much as he can in order to use as little of the world's limited resources as possible. He is not reliant upon external energy, food or water supplies but produces everything he needs on his own land.

In his books, he wants to share the theoretical and practical knowledge that he has gained over many years on the subject with the widest range of readers possible. He cannot change anything alone but if only a little of his philosophy of permaculture is practised by the broad public, he has done his part in improving the relationship between people and nature for many years to come.

PREFACE

Permaculture is a concept for providing sustainable, long-term environmental cycles and is rooted in the observation of nature and its natural patterns. It is both a science and an art of biomimicry. Biomimicry is a science which is based on the observation of nature and which develops solutions for mankind. Nature is the ultimate architect which continues to develop in this complex universe. This is very important for us, our planet and our homes. Without the universe, we would not be able to live on Earth.

Nature is not only beautiful but is also shockingly efficient in it form and function. When one thing is formed, it strengthens something else. Nothing is "useless" in nature. Everything has its role. For example, the reason that proteins work in a particular way is simply due to their structural form. Muscle cells are layers of elongated fibres which can contract and expand. The beauty of flowers attracts insects on which pollen attaches itself. In this way the pollen can reach new areas and reproduce with other plants.

The most common example of biomimicry and permaculture is the well-known velcro fastener, which was invented by a Swiss engineer. He removed the natural burs from his dog's fur and noticed how the fine hooks of the burs stuck on to the fur. Another good example is better packaging designs. Have you ever considered what natural packaging could look like? Try imagining pomegranate seeds inside a pomegranate. It helps us understand how efficient the system is. What we can learn from permaculture is basically the art of biomimicry: observing the most effective designs of Nature and using its principles.

Permaculture is a complete system design with a sophisticated methodology. It is a set of sustainable principles, for use in our environment. It is derived from nature and is applicable to everything which we create and design. In the words of the architect, William McDonough: "Design is the first signal of human intention"[1]. When we observe the ecosystems in nature, we see that every animal gives to our environment and takes from it. They eat and breathe. They breathe out and excrete waste so that nutrients can return to their natural surroundings. Plants take nutrients from that and release them in the form of sugar and other compounds. Everything has its use and when it all works together; it paints a wonderful picture of a healthy and balanced ecosystem.

---

[11] The Hannover Principles: "Design for Sustainability", from the 2012 20th Anniversary Printing, November 2012

We are learning that what we take from the world is given back in another form. "Regenerative design" refers to a way of creating designs which should give back to nature what it has taken. Permaculture is based, for the most part, on regenerative design. As such, we can take permaculture out of being solely ecological landscaping and incorporate it into the world of industry, production, finances or even state structures. Accomplishing that would enable us to live and appreciate our world of regenerative design to its fullest extent. At present, many of our buildings and automobiles are limited to their function instead of care being taken about their form. Their function tends to cause unbelievable amounts of damage to our world. Instead, we could work with regenerative design. Would it not be wonderful if our buildings and automobiles could filter water and at the same time improve air quality? If we could replenish the environment, our world could be a wonderfully clean place.

How exactly does permaculture change the world? On the one hand, permaculture can change deserts into productive oases which produce food. The world-renowned permaculturist, Geoff Lawton, changed the deserts of Jordan Valley into a wonderland, in just a few years. He captured the water and stored it, introduced drip irrigation and planted bushes and important fruit trees next to it. The trees draw from the water which is stored in the ground, so it needs no external water. Because a variety of trees was planted, there is no necessity for the use of additional resources.

Initially, nutrients were added from external sources, but within a few years, so much water had collected in the ground that even fungi started to grow. The trees provided food for the local community and turned the desert from a rough, barren environment into a lush, life-supporting ecosystem.

One excellent example of applied permaculture design is the storage of rain water and waste water recycling. Drinking water is one of the biggest challenges of the twenty-first century. Water is plentiful, but up to now, we have not been developing our systems efficiently. The desert around San Diego is low on rainwater resources. For that reason, the inhabitants of the area catch rainwater and store it on their roofs – that is typical for a suburban house in that climatic zone. A total of around 25,000 litres of water is collected per year – and that with only about 5 cm rain per year in the desert.

Imagine combining that with an intelligent waste water design. Waste water could be gained, mainly through activities, such as washing, dishwashing and bathing. By the principles of permaculture, that water would be recycled locally, resulting in water, which has been used once but is only lightly contaminated. It could easily be filtered, purified and re-used locally – and that endlessly.

In other words, we could do our laundry in the water which we have used to wash our hands, once it has been filtered. When we have done the laundry, we can use the same water to water our plants, etc. This way we could dramatically reduce the amount of water we use at home, possibly by half.

If you combine that with the rainwater and its storage, we could almost live self-sufficiently as far as water usage is concerned, particularly if we were to implement other permaculture designs. Compost toilets and water-saving taps could save even more water. If we are clever with our water design, there is really no necessity to adjust to the idea of water shortage due to climate change.

Einstein once said that problems cannot be solved with the same thoughts which caused them. This is also true of permaculture. Permaculture is a completely new way of thinking. We must not only search for the solutions which are found in nature, but also from the perspective of using a suitable system. As ever, the symptoms are not the main cause of the problem.

The examples of fruit trees, rainwater and water recycling, mentioned above, are only a few of the many possibilities of permaculture design. Our modern civilisation has always fought to gain control over nature. We have tried to reduce and mechanise nature. We have used resources without consideration of its implications to the ecosystem. Now we have reached the point in history where we must learn how to form a partnership with nature. We must regard it as our ally, otherwise we are heading for catastrophe.

From a distance, our behaviour seems like a yeast mould or a cancer cell which after using all available resources in its environment, continues to grow. Once the resources have been used up there is nothing left but death and decay.

WHAT IS PERMACULTURE?

The main aim of permaculture is regeneration. The harmonious and ecological relationship between humans and their planet would create a world where there would be enough food, water, accommodation and opportunity for creativity for everyone. It sounds like an ambitious aim, but it provides the potential for us to regain our fantastic, flourishing and abundant world.

We spoke about permaculture as biomimicry in the previous chapter and about regenerative design which promotes expansion. Permaculture is a wide-ranging concept for our society and the world. Everything in permaculture is based on a series of quintessential ethical and design principles. Just as a tree grows towards the sky and has roots, permaculture penetrates deep into the earth.

It follows an idealistic vision because it requires its ethical values to be as deeply rooted as its principles. The ethical basis ensures that the technology we create from our ideal visions is built on strong foundations. The ethos of permaculture is unbelievably simple and fascinatingly effective. It cares about people, cares about earth and ensures that surpluses are shared.

We care for people by taking care of people. We should use our human abilities to work towards a safe, more regenerative future. Permaculture possesses tremendous power which people need to produce ecological sustainability. Our human creativity has too often been used for destructive purposes. However, the same energy can be used for regeneration and sustainability purposes.

Humans have lived for many thousands of years on the earth. As our population grew, so did its ability to destroy. It is clear that we are now at a crossroad, a turning point where we could use this opportunity to heal our planet.

Beyond ecological design, permaculture encompasses a whole realm of life philosophy. It recognises the decisive role we all have to play. People must step up and do their part in achieving this global vision in order to achieve health and sustainability.

LOOKING AFTER PLANET EARTH

We cannot live without a healthy planet. We have evolved over millions of years to adjust to the biogeographic climate of our planet. Therefore, it is unlikely that we could colonise another planet at short notice.

If we were to see ourselves as the custodians of the earth, we could extend our time here significantly. Therefore, it is important to be active in the development of technology and regenerative practices which not only heal our planet but also maximise the ecology, which would be beneficial in fulfilling our needs.

It sounds like a tall order but it brings everything into perspective. It helps us to orientate, make decisions about design and other actions we take towards that end.

SHARING OUR SURPLUSES

This idea seems radical and some people compare it even with communism or socialism. It is, indeed, nothing short of a radical form of redistribution. In actual fact, it has nothing to do with that. We just have to recognise the necessity to take care of both mankind and the planet. Of course, this means that we must share the fruits of our work in order to preserve the health and happiness of all living things.

The present global consumption behaviour of capitalism causes such an imbalance that rich nations are using the resources of several planets, while the disadvantaged nations sink into poverty. Permaculture rejects this imbalance in favour of balance. We have enough resources for everyone if we share our surpluses.

During the whole process we are specifically attempting to design durable systems because that is the only good and feasible path to take for our future. This means we must grow enough food to feed not only ourselves but also our neighbours.

We must never forget that this all means hard work. For this reason, while designing our target system we must always take care that we consider the multitude of inter-personal relationships necessary for success. Durable systems which are based on good relationships, ensure that we shall never suffer shortages. Should we have a shortage, we should have access to the surpluses of the greater community.

Permaculture is basically a philosophy which brings all elements into an ideal relationship. Social permaculture is particularly important when practising active regenerative sustainability.

Everyone has been in a difficult situation sometime and has needed help to get out of the crisis. This ethos recognises that such a solidarity principle is the key to a peaceful and happy community. It is, therefore, desirable that where surpluses of food occur, they would be shared with those whose harvests were less successful. Not only because it is a nice thing to do, but also because we are all parts of the same world and our resilience is dependent upon having a sense of community. Our own happiness next year could be dependent upon whether our neighbours had been less successful this year and we were able to help them.

This returns us to the creation of sustainability through the correct balance of mankind and nature. The whole permaculture ethos can be condensed into the following sentence: "Care for the Earth; care for mankind; share your surpluses".

This highlights the cyclical ethos that mankind is the caretaker of the earth. If we manage our activities on this world with caution, we help it to thrive instead of harming it. This way we can do our part in leaving behind, with pride not shame, a world which our children and grandchildren can inherit. Permaculture may not be the remedy for every sickness of this society but every day it becomes more obvious that we must change something, and quickly. In the short-term we can break through the cycle of destruction. Violence between people and against the planet is avoidable.

Let us take a deeper look into the principles of permaculture and see how we can create a new world, something that mankind has always longed for.

HOW DOES PERMACULTURE WORK?

Permaculture embodies the key principles of "how everything works in Nature". These principles are the basis and the building bricks of life itself. In the following pages we will learn about each of the building bricks, individually. Together they form a harmonious coexistence with this planet – a coexistence where each part receives as much as it gives.

WATCHING AND INTERACTING

If we take the time to think about nature, we can create design solutions which fit to our personal needs. Our world has a wealth of landscapes, terrains and climate zones which is a unique opportunity and challenge for us. We humans have proven ourselves to be extremely adaptable but we tend to be destroyers too, perhaps due to a lack of knowledge rather than wilfulness.

We have changed the landscape forever and adapted the natural paths of our drinking water to suit our needs. We are used to modern comforts which at present would not be available without using expensive and environmental unfriendly resources.

We should study the world around us more consciously and intensively in order to recognise how indigenous organisms interact with each other. In the environment we can find many, if not all, the solutions we need to survive and thrive. For example, people often laugh at igloos, but because of their dome-like construction they are extremely efficient to heat and offer excellent protection from wind and weather.

In order to understand our natural surroundings, we need to study carefully how indigenous creatures were created to best live in their particular environment and how they interact with it. As soon as we know how this is done, we can copy it ourselves, using modern science and technology. It is possible to condition land areas to be suitable for farming, even in such harsh climate zones as Death Valley or the barren Mojave Desert.

In such places, many indigenous, edible plants can be farmed which are suitable for the local people. This leads to a less hostile and more balanced ecosystem in which humans and nature can work together. These are conditions which would benefit everyone and everything.

The key to understanding our nature is to observe it. Nature is simple, not good or bad, wise or foolish. There are no reference frameworks in nature. Our personal judgment and prejudices separate us from nature and impede our designs. The most important starting point for understanding our environment is to view it with an impartial eye.

If we tread the same path as we have always done, we will never recognise new things that we did not previously notice: A small sparrow, a bird's nest, an ant colony and much more which was long hidden from us.

If we slow down our lifestyles, we begin to notice changes in our microclimate and recognise the structure of the geography around us. The more intimately we deal with them, the more familiar we will become with them. Building a relationship with the land is essential for permaculture design. If we watch animals for a while, we will quickly realise that.

You too should observe your own habitat. We learn from what others have observed and we should try to act accordingly – living in harmony with our own environment. If everyone observes their own terrain and bases their design tools on their observations, this system can be used throughout the world. Every climate has its own challenges and demands and has its own abilities to preserve life. Of course, the challenges of the desert are very different from those in the Swiss Alps. In the same way, the rain forests offer different possibilities to the tundra. For this reason, observation and understanding are at the core of permaculture.

Indigenous creatures and plants show us a lot about the best ways to use the resources of the area, sustainably. For example, if you take the time to observe the animals in your vicinity, you will quickly notice what you can learn by observation. Communication, wisdom and evolutionary growth is around us all the time. Everything you see is connected to every other form of life.

If you have seen the world-famous film "AVATAR" in the cinema, you could see with your own eyes how we should live with nature. This is exactly how it works with our earthly existence and the nature which surrounds us. Nature has its own dynamic culture and we should not try to exclude or interfere with its processes. If we adjust to the idea that we must adapt our lifestyle completely, we grow ourselves and ensure a life of harmony with our surroundings.

With the great strides we have taken in almost all disciplines and sciences, it is possible to create sustainable living conditions over nearly the whole world. The more we commit ourselves to the needs of nature without changing it, the healthier we will make the world and the healthier those will be who live in it.

GENERATING AND STORING ENERGY

We are able to produce energy easily due to the development of systems which collect resources. It is not necessary to go without our computers or electrical equipment. Energy is plentiful and we can use it, in times of need, without problems.

Nature provides us with an abundance of energy, sun, water, seeds, minerals, heat, wind and organic substances. We could save ourselves a lot of toil and sweat if we were to take the path of least resistance: For example, storing solar energy when the sun is high and shining strongly, installing rainwater collection systems for storing water or using stones to store warmth. Making compost to enable organic farming is also a classical and well-tried way to farm efficiently.

If we craft our methods to harmonise with nature, we will dramatically simplify our work.

We have the technology to generate power. What we need is the facility for storing sustainable energy. Plants could be our greatest inspiration in this. Every plant cell contains a huge water store. Trees branch out in the so-called fibonacci-spiral, so that they can collect unlimited amounts of water from the ground. If we were to calculate the amount of sunlight which falls on each leaf, it quickly becomes clear how solar energy is created and stored.

If we were to build our energy requirements on the "capture and storage system" like the tree, we could become infinitely more efficient and regenerative. Artificial photosynthesis is already possible. The next step is to be able to imitate the storage of plant energy. Wind, rain, sun and geotherms are all present in one form or another almost all the time.

Our most important task is to use the energy when it is available and be in a position to save it in times of need so that we can live self-sufficiently. Sustainable energy forms must therefore be created realistically and practically and this is easier now that it has ever been.

ACHIEVING A YIELD

Ensure that you receive a really useful reward for your work. Essentially, you are relieved when you have a good harvest and perhaps even receive a small profit. However, a healthy harvest is not only achieving copiously sprouting vegetable crops. A good harvest also includes ensuring the provision of electricity and water in the house and having the ability to use modern amenities in an ecologically sustainable way.

Contrary to popular opinion, permaculture does not seek to remove technology or to propagate a primitive lifestyle. Instead it should combine technology and ecology in order to achieve their maximum potentials.

As your own producer, you should be able to generate sufficient yield and you will also be providing added value to the eco-system. If you are able to produce more food than you really need, there are countless ways to store it for leaner times.

Surpluses can also be used as exchange items for goods or services which you would not normally receive. This way, a sustainable economy can be fuelled which is dependent upon the work of its individuals. This is not only simple to achieve and practical, it is also a very beneficial lifestyle.

On the other hand, the surplus crops can be used to make compost which can be used as fertilizer for the next season. That invigorates and regenerates the tired earth. Any surplus which you do not need for your household, and which cannot be stored, can be offered to a third party as a gift. In this way you can take care of your neighbours and share the surplus meaningfully. If everyone used the basic principles of permaculture, we could create a stable society where everyone receives their fair share of the proceeds and a reasonable return for their efforts.

This way, it is possible to develop a continual, self-sustaining cycle which fulfils the require-ments of everyone.

SELF REGULATING AND RESPONDING

Nature is normally able to regulate imbalances in the eco-system. One example of that is the ratio of deer and wolves. Deer breed where there is a lot of food for them. Too many deer will lead to a reduction in greenery available, which in turn will prevent new greenery growth. Then the wolves come and find an unbelievable number of deer in the area. The wolves eat the deer and increase the numbers in their pack, at the same time reducing the deer population. Once the deer population has reduced to a certain level, the wolves will move on to a new area. The plants recover, completing the cycle and starting it again from the beginning.

If we accept the signals from our own environment, one thing will become abundantly clear: What we are doing is not advantageous. The signals from nature are a warning that we are doing something wrong and we must change something. This is why we could reasonably expect that everyone would work together in unison with our world.

Everywhere cultures collide, each having its own agenda, which will inevitably affect others. The natural world is the stage of many conflicts. Mankind seems to have given very little consideration to nature. The key to successful preservation is to understand that everything we do influences our world. By self-regulating our behaviour, we can craft our environment naturally and logically so that it can regenerate and repair what has been damaged.

In the history of mankind, it has often been seen as personal and negative feedback when people speak about the warning signs of nature. However, this is not a judgment, it is an imbalance in our eco-system and it is in our interests to take on this challenge. If we react to the warning signs, we can ensure that we have the correct relationship to Mother Earth.

USING RENEWABLE RESOURCES

Toxic vapours from factories adversely affect plants. The depletion of our rain forests and the myriads of life forms intensify the environmental pollution with shocking dynamism. In addition, modern practices such as wholesale slaughtering, and the fights between humans for the rights of oil, coal and precious metals, have added to the problem. The world is in turmoil over things which, if evenly distributed, would be sufficient for everyone.

Nature has given us everything we need to survive. Our intellect is probably the best tool for cultivating and adapting our environment to suit our needs.

The difficulty does not lie in the fact that we use natural resources, but in the fact that we do almost nothing to replenish them or to replace non-renewable resources with renewable ones, which offer the same results.

As humans we have the ability and the capacity to change our environment in a way that no other creature on the earth can. This is why we have a much greater responsibility to the world to use renewable resources and services.

AVOID PRODUCING WASTE

If we make use of all our resources, nothing will go to waste. What we throw away is often regarded by Mother Nature as a valuable resource. Urine and excrement are considered "waste". In reality, these by-products of digestion are excellent fertilisers. These so-called by-products are rich in nitrogen, which the plants need to grow. Nitrogen is extremely useful for all forms of plant cultures. Our lifestyle has led us to an unnatural conclusion. The present concept is: Produce waste.

We often compete to achieve more than we can practically use or actually need, from paper to plastic cups.

We do not care about - or think about - the damage we cause to our environment. Some kinds of paper cups are made using various toxic substances. But what happens to them when they arrive at the waste disposal site? What happens when these toxic substances are released into the ground and mix over the years with the battery acids and other synthetic materials? This mixture of poisonous material ends up over time in our groundwater. For this reason, waste disposal sites are truly a slow and painful way of poisoning.

This is not good for the water which we rely on to survive. In addition, the sites release Carbon Dioxide and Methane into the atmosphere and serve to increase the greenhouse gases which are already there. Methane is more than twenty times more efficient at absorbing radiation than carbon. This makes it a much more deadly greenhouse gas. Nature does not produce waste. It is normal for us humans to throw things away but in truth there is no real "away". It is not "away", it is only on another part of our Earth.

In nature, "waste" is nourishment for new growth. In the cycle of life, death is a necessary part of the evolution of the Earth. If we rethink our definition of "waste" to mean resource, we can consider creating materials which can somehow be recycled or composted at the end of a year. We have much to learn about recycling. We have made big strides but our methods are crude, time-consuming and hopelessly primitive in comparison to the subtle and efficient methods which nature has developed.

The integration of molecular recycling would enable us to tap into a huge reserve of seemingly irretrievable materials and recycle them for new uses. It means creating new ways. By studying the reaction of nature on various forms of waste, from animal carcasses to computer casing, we can learn much about how to deal best with them and adapt the knowledge for our own use.

DESIGN OF PATTERNS TO THE SMALLEST DETAIL

Patterns and models are to be found everywhere in nature. All are made for specific purposes. The double-helix pattern, for example, that is inherent in the DNA of every living creature on our planet, can determine the purple striped pattern on the back of every coral snake or the pattern of seeds inside a pine cone. Nature is practically nothing other than patterns.

An example of that is the striking spiral architecture of the shell of a nautilus. The shell that the mollusc grows - or builds - is an ideal construction to sustain its life. It contains everything it needs to grow and thrive. Nothing more, nothing less.

A short while ago, engineering students from Teheran, Iran, built a building based on the nautilus shell. They discovered that the building not only provided shelter but also, to a certain extent, regulated itself. They thought that it would be most unlikely, if not downright impossible. This achievement was rewarded by giving the group the "Prestige Sustainable Design Award" and they also received international acclaim for their project. While they were observing the nautilus shell, they discovered that there is a vast human desire for natural habitats. This created an enormous social breakthrough on this subject.

This type of adaption does not need to be restricted to its original environment. Imagine, for example, that we knew exactly how the muscles of an ant work. These busy little insects have unbelievable strength in comparison to their size.

Using patterns to our advantage, we can protect - and at the same time use - our infinitely precious resources. We could, for example, use crystalline matrices for data storage which are much more efficient than the clumsy binary/magnetic systems that we have to use at present.

However, in order to understand them, we must get to know their pattern. Nature has already taken the first step. We must now learn to work with them effectively. However, knowledge of the pattern is only the first step. We must then introduce the changes ourselves. Although many of these patterns cannot be effectively used without people, we ourselves can make a difference if we begin to change ourselves.

If we do not, we risk sacrificing our basic principles. That is like calculating a zero sum or even worse: It is like a lost equation within its innate nature; one that is capable of giving form and structure to every facet of our universe. Thus, the infinite dance of the atoms is maintained right up to the majestic rotations in the galaxies of our universe. Using these patterns, together with human effort, we can construct excellent, sustainable methods and tools.

INTEGRATE NOT SEPARATE

You can master integration instead of separation when you bring the right things to the right places, develop relationships between things and work together to support each other. Separation is not normally a natural phenomenon. Things which are similar tend to stick together. But there is also a complex relationship between seemingly dissimilar things.

What, for example, does a small black beetle have to do with a horse? Superficially, the answer does not seem to be obvious. Dung beetles use horse manure as nourishment, shelter and birthing station for their babies. The same can be said for the relationship between one of the smallest creatures on earth, the almost microscopic plankton and the largest creature of the sea, the majestic blue whale.

The blue whale has a very fine filter which enables it to scoop up tons of plankton, thus creating a pairing between them. Surely this must be one of the strangest pairings, but looking at it from a superficial level, it is a pairing of the natural world.

A more common example is the relationship between horse and man. Tamed horses are reliant upon humans. They have to be groomed and fed. Humans use horses for sport, work, transport and food. You can probably imagine many other examples. The point is that, if dissimilar elements are brought together, then both parties can profit from each other. This is the obvious part of the cooperation.

Elements complement each other and can be advantageous to both sides. Instead of separating plants in different blocks, which is typical in large-scale farming, one could consider the interplay between the elements.

Permaculture prefers the so-called interplanting-system. A diversity of plants benefits from its mutual advantages when sharing nutrition, which, in turn, enhances the diversity of insects and microbes, while building up resilience against outbreaks of sickness within the eco-system.

Study carefully your own environment and introduce prudent elements instead of destructive ones. Only humans can work towards creating natural relationships which improve the environment and encourage diversity.

History is full of examples of times and situations when humans have introduced (either through carelessness, thoughtlessness or simple ignorance) non-indigenous species into a biosphere which have consequently spread like wildfire. A particular form of Japanese beetle is an alarming example of this. This pest came to America onboard a ship and began to multiply at an alarming rate as soon as it reached the shore. Today, this beetle is directly responsible for millions of dollars of damage to the farmland and trees. Without its natural enemy, the beetle population is almost impossible to keep in check. People are becoming more and more desperate in their attempts to remove it and often resort to using strong chemicals. The cycle of predator and prey, producer and consumer are one of the basic necessities of nature. We should not change it artificially.

Through appropriate relationships we cultivate links to our own world by helping to maintain a healthy and blossoming ecology. We create a world which does not only support ourselves, but also the plants and animals upon which we are dependent, in many ways. They need our resources because we draw on their resources. Integration and working for the community at large are not only advantageous aims in the short-term but also sensible ones in the long-term. However, we must first understand how things relate to each other before we can find really practical solutions.

We have to be absolutely sure that a multifariously integrated system is developed with health in mind. It must be measured, justified and carefully controlled. Introduction and integration of these measures will prove much more sustainable than the constant extraction of nourishment from the earth. Equally, on the subject of social and financial aspects, our systems are more robust when there is provision for various perspectives and abilities, as well as the generation of diverse cash flows. More diversity is followed by more flexibility. That is the law of nature.

SET YOURSELF SMALL, SLOW SOLUTIONS

Small, slow solutions are easier to maintain than large, cumbersome ones because they can be achieved sustainably using local resources. Some humans are impatient. They demand immediate satisfaction. Everything must be available quickly, must be bigger or stronger.

These days we only seem to need an internet connection to make a latte, preferably with artificial sweetener. Because of this desire for "more" we have effectively excluded nature. Because of this, we are denying ourselves the benefits of a slower, simpler lifestyle with greater rewards. Nature does not begin on a grand scale when it is forming a new system. A hurricane starts with a simple swirl of warm air above cold water and, despite that, can grow and develop into a destructive force.

As mentioned before, nature does not allow waste. This makes it much more efficient in finding solutions for mankind. It uses the smallest, slowest and simplest solutions to create the desired effects. People tend to think in large dimensions. Of course, a snowflake or corn seed cannot create a great effect. However, it is possible that a snowflake can trigger an avalanche, and a corn seed can eventually feed a whole village if it is well tended and allowed to develop into a plant.

Small systems do not produce the same dynamic as large, artificial systems, of course. However, in general they work better and more efficiently. Drip systems that the farmers use today, which offer an alternative to the traditional irrigation techniques, are a good example of this. In contrast to that, large, traditional irrigation systems waste so much more water than is necessary to produce the harvest. Water drip systems deliver continuous water where it is needed. Because it works more slowly and has the aim of maintaining plant health while, at the same time, not straining the water resources. This leaves more water for the livestock and for human consumption.

These days, sustainability and conservation are equated with lowering of the standard of living. However, if we mimic the way that nature resolves all of its problems, the same kind of problems that we are confronted with, we can learn how to use less resources. Effective methods to achieve greater benefits are available to all of us.

In our own lives, and in our social structures, we tend to expect things to happen overnight. Unfortunately, this is not how our natural world works. It is absolutely essential to implement small and slow changes. Realise the transformation of complete systems to realise your expectations of permaculture!

UTILISATION AND DIVERSITY

Diversity reduces the vulnerability of many endangered species and uses the uniqueness of the environment in which it exists. Biodiversity is a very hot topic at the moment. You can see, hear and read the many discussions on this subject.

When we think of diversity, we think of skin colour, political orientation, religious or philosophical convictions, sexual and gender orientation and many other recognisable differences.

Nature defines diversity in a much larger way. Think for a moment about the species of plants and animals which live in a specific area. There is a natural balance within it. Plants may not grow too wildly or they will try to displace or kill each other in their efforts to survive. Animals must eat the plants, but without natural enemies they are in danger of over-breeding and destroying their own food resources.

For this reason, nature has developed its own food chain and eco-system which can transform even barren areas into oases. Plants feed from the nutrition and bacteria in the ground and then themselves fall prey to the nutritional needs of other animals, which themselves fall victim to larger animals and so on. The biological diversity of an area can be as simple as three or four steps or as complex as many thousands of mathematical operations. In both cases the end result is the same. Diversity also involves strengthening the lower levels of the chain and introducing new types of plants and animals which can resist diseases.

Some time ago, a group of scientists genetically modified a type of grain so that it would produce extraordinary yields, resulting in a surplus which far exceeded normal yields.

A number of farmers agreed to plant the grain. The result was that this new grain attracted an excessive number of a particular type of insect. After a short while, the fields were decimated. The farmers did not take the grain for very long and after a while the whole project was shelved. In comparison, standard cultures do not suffer from that kind of problem.

The moral of the story is clear: Diversity equates to life, while uniformity can often mean death. The more diverse a region and its species are, the more likely the region is to survive, even under the most extreme conditions. This way, a variety of foodstuffs can not only be maintained but a healthy eco-system is supported and certain foods are protected from diseases, pests or predators. In addition, it is easier for our world and its inhabitants to ensure that, with care, healthy competition and evolution can take place. This can happen with or without our intervention.

USE THE MARGINAL BOUNDARIES

Boundaries are separations between two systems. The border between these two systems is called a transitional zone. An example of such a boundary in permaculture is the transition between forest and pasture. It is in these transitional zones that you find the lushest forms of life on the planet. The reason for this is that life forms of two different systems which can be found in these regions (i.e. two systems that share a border). Where there is a mixture between one system and another, plants, animals and humans have the opportunity to interact and influence each other. Understanding how these reactions occur and how they can be used, forms a large part of permaculture. Here, in these regions, there is the greatest potential for change and energy generation. Wind and metal do not seem to have much in common at first sight. However, when the metal has the right form and angle to catch the wind, it can produce energy for any number of uses. It can be used to mill grain or to produce enough electrical energy for you to be able to read this book. The same applies to other methods of power generation.

If we understand the role that marginal boundaries play and interact with each other, we are in the perfect position to be able to copy these complex relationships of nature for our own use. If we use this ability correctly, we can be the agents of change. It can help us restore the imbalance which our current destructive behaviour has caused and find a way back to a sustainable, regenerative culture.

This understanding results in more than just superficial advantages. If we create our own boundaries and interactions, we can influence the world around us and often tread unexpected paths. It is important that that we are careful when we begin to blur the boundaries, that we do not mistakenly eradicate something which could be the key to our survival.

We should not plunge into making changes to things, just because we can. Instead, we must study concepts which can be used gently, economically and only when necessary. Too often in human history we have interfered in the biospheres of "new" areas, only to leave behind unforeseen destruction in our natural environments.

Sustainable living means developing an understanding for the area we live in. When we understand how everything is related to everything else, we have the chance to find a way of life that most other people would consider to be inconceivable. It is tangibly simple.

BE CREATIVE TO MAKE SIGNIFICANT CHANGES

In the words of the Greek Philosopher, Heraclitus: "Change is the only constant in life". We can positively influence changes through careful observation and timely intervention. This particular principle of permaculture is a logical conclusion; an inevitable conclusion which can have the most important of results.

All of these concepts are as inextricably linked as any food chain. If you take a link out of the chain, you risk collapsing the whole system. Permaculture urges us to react to these changes with creativity.

The fundamentally positive ethic of perma-culture means that we should lead our culture back into a self-sustaining cycle. No-one is served by reacting out of fear. Earth looks after the people and shares the surplus. We must do this also.

This principle also applies to our personal life and our institutional structures. Many people do not believe in change. Such life-changing transitions can mean shifts in identity and self-perception. If we can accept that these changes are inevitable, but also offer us a chance to learn, grow and develop our awareness, the changes will not be felt as strongly. It is easy to react with fear and guilt if our culture, climate or environment change, but it is more important to accept the conditions and find creative, positive solutions.

PRACTICAL EXAMPLES OF THE USE OF PERMACULTURE

Now that we have spoken about the overriding philosophy, core ethics and principles of permaculture, we will now look at some basic techniques and their correct usage:

These include:

- Natural building

- The choice of suitable building materials

- The recycling of rain and grey water

- Composting

- Permaculture garden

We will deal with all these techniques in detail on the following pages.

NATURAL BUILDING

A typical and well-known example of near-natural building is the cob style house, seen in several places in Devonshire, South England, which are made of clay and straw, trodden by oxen. It is known that these structures can stand for more than a hundred years with only minimum repairs necessary. Contrary to the general opinion, these structures survive particularly well. It is unbelievable to see what the earth offers. Not only does our nutrition grow naturally to feed the diverse lifeforms of the earth, but our planet created also remarkable building materials for us.

Today, our buildings and houses are made from a mixture of concrete, wood, synthetic and other materials. Synthetic materials can generally not be recycled into nature again. Some parts can be recycled or re-used but the majority finds its way to the waste disposal sites. We love our big, shiny skyscrapers and modern architecture, but they serve to pollute our planet and cause more waste than necessary.

Due to increasing energy and living costs, a global recession and growing concern for our environment, there has been a revival of interest in natural building. Natural building fits perfectly into the principles of permaculture. It values renewable energy, resources and services. It captures energy and stores it, producing no waste products. Earth-based structures are cheap to build because earth, clay and water can be sourced close-by. You just need to dig up the earth close to the house.

CHOOSING SUITABLE BUILDING MATERIALS

Natural buildings ensure efficient insulation. They stay warm during cold winters and are cool in hot summers. They need wood or metal roofs for protection against water but otherwise they last for generations before they need to be repaired. Building a house from earth and mud demands that we must work the earth, water and hay and bring it into the required form. It is not a job for one person alone, we have to do it together. Inviting a larger community to help with the building of a new house and the cooperation necessary for natural building brings communities together with the earth and demonstrates the core ethic of permaculture in its purest form.

Natural building does not only refer to the construction of ecologically sustainable houses and other buildings, it also offers spiritual and psychological advantages. The nature which our ancestors developed, included no right-angles, straight surfaces, monochrome colours or stiff uniformity. Most modern houses lack diversity, form, colour and structure, and therefore do not stimulate our senses.

It is possible to give natural buildings a shape, as long as the moist earth can be formed. The organic curvatures of natural buildings promote our natural creativity and connect us to the forms and patterns of nature. If you do not like the organic curvature of the cob walls you can choose a more modern form, using compressed earth, incorporating right-angled edges and straight, flat walls. There is more than one type of earth-wall. There are various materials to choose from, including cob, adobe, earth bags, straw balls and compressed earth. Choosing one of these, you can design and build your natural building just as you like it.

Cob is one of the most-loved natural building materials, made with earth, clay, water and straw. Modern-day cob structures are creative in form, including smooth and curving walls, decorated with upcycled glass, coloured stones and rocks and even paintings in plaster. Cob walls, decorated with glass mosaic are unbelievably beautiful, as are the addition of glass windows. The great thing about cob is that it stems from one of the simplest techniques of natural building which needs no firing of bricks, no formwork or design forms.

Adobe buildings are extremely durable, being found in some of the oldest civilisations in the world, even older than the tiles which were used in mud-brick houses. Decorative designs on single tiles can still be integrated into today's buildings. Earthbags are made of a mixture of earth and straw in corn sacks which are piled up like bricks. They are covered by clay or plaster in order to drain water or prevent damage from the climate or the sun's rays. Compressed earth is more complicated than necessary. A moist mixture of sand, gravel and clay is pressed into a wooden form either to make a solid earthen wall or to make individual bricks. Limestone can also be added as a stabiliser.

Architect, Michael Reynolds, became widely-known for his invention of the "Earthship Biotecture Community" which used earth-based and recycled materials to build houses. Old car tyres were used, as an example, as supporting structures for walls. Old wine and beer bottles and other discarded materials were embedded in the earth and were used as decoration and supports. The "Reynold's Experiment", as it was known, originated in New Mexico with the idea of building structures using recycled waste materials. In the meantime, a community of young people has developed, spanning the whole world, who advise and educate in the building of natural houses.

RECYCLING OF GREY WATER

Did you know that rainwater can be harvested? It is possible to save up to 50% of the average use of grey water by re-using it? But what is grey water? Basically, grey water is nothing other than faecal-free, lightly soiled waste water, such as you would find after showering, bathing, hand-washing or that which comes out of the washing machine. At first sight, that number may seem astonishing when we comprehend how important water is for our health and well-being of our planet.

Through the construction of intelligent water systems, we can reduce the amount of water we use by half, without compromises.

In permaculture, household waste water is divided into two groups:

1. Grey water refers to the waste water from our showers, washing machines and washbasins. It contains bacteria, fibre particles and dead skin cells, which are even nutritious to the earth and do not pose a health risk.

2. Black water refers to the waste water from our toilets and wash basins, and could be contaminated with faeces or fat. It can contain animal parasites or Nitrogen, which pollute the environment.

Grey water can be fed directly into your garden, while black water needs a much more thorough filtering before it returns to the ecosystem. In permaculture we use special systems to harvest rainwater in rainwater catchment areas. After all, rainwater falls free of charge from the sky and is a part of our natural water circulation. The use of rainwater also significantly reduces the amount of water that we draw from our reservoirs or from the earth's surface.

Rainwater is astonishing because it is naturally soft, free from chlorine and other chemicals which are present in our tap water, and it saves money, which can be seen on your water bills. Rainwater is very simple to harvest. All you need is a slanting roof, guttering and a downpipe which leads to your storage container. To be on the safe side, you need a mosquito net, a lid and a hosepipe and your rain collector is complete. If you want to collect even more rainwater from your roof, you can arrange several storage devices in a row and connect the storage tanks using a pipe. You can use your rainwater for drinking, watering your garden or you can connect it to your house water installation. The best use of your grey water is for watering your plants.

If you keep your water in a tank, solid particles can be incorporated, so that they sink to the bottom and prevent your pipes from blockage. This is optimal. However, it means that the tank needs to be pumped out once a year. You can recycle these solids in your composting system without worry.

A well-known permaculture farm in Australia has a very sophisticated mulch pit next to the grey water system, where the grey water from the washing machine is pumped directly into various mulch columns. You could plant a nice, shady tree next to your mulch pit which would be a useful source of nutrition for people and animals, biomass for compost, fuel and many other things. This way, you would also be planning for the future of companion plants which could be planted near to the tree. Companion plants are those which profit from each other by being close together.

COMPOSTING

Did you know that your compost can be used for other things besides fertilizing your garden? It can also be used to control soil erosion, to suppress plant diseases, to filter rainwater and even to generate heat and electricity. Compost absorbs rain and prevents it from washing out the soil. It is also full of micro-organisms which are known for their bio-controlling properties.

Bio-controlling organisms combat pathogens and are effective antibiotic, antimycotic and parasitism agents. Coarse compost can be used as a filter in rain gardens. Toxic metals and inorganic acids remain in the humus (the end-product of composting), allowing clean water to flow through.

If you have never heard of Jean Pain, you should definitely look at his work on YouTube. He was a French innovator who produced 100% of his energy needs through his compost system. He collected storm wood and put it through a wood chipper, making a huge pile. He built a complete infrastructure of water hosepipes through the inside of the pile and installed an anaerobic digester in the middle of the pile.

The Methane which was produced was used to run his electricity generator, was used for cooking and to refuel his lorry. Jean Pain was innovative. Recently, interest in his systems has begun to re-kindle and more and more compost heat-recovery systems are appearing. If there is anything in nature which embodies regenerative potential, it is decomposition. In the natural eco-system leaves, sticks, dead insects and microbes fall to the ground. A little water and a little Oxygen encourage life to develop underground.

The universe revels in the gifts of death. The earth's food network reaches from single-cell bacteria up to multi-cell insects and even larger animals, such as earthworms and beetles. It is the activities of all these earth organisms, which feast and then excrete, which in turn produce nutrients as soon as they are released into the soil. In permaculture we often leave flowers, leaves, fruits and sticks to rot, which decay where they have grown. This produces a lush mulch bed which contains other nutrients and can at some point be introduced to the plants to help with their growth.

THE PERMACULTURE GARDEN – ZONES AND SECTORS

It can be a daunting prospect to turn a wild or empty piece of land into a functioning permaculture garden. The good news is that there are two techniques which can help to ease the design process. They are known as zones and sectors. Zones are based on the premise of reducing time and energy. Plants are zoned, depending on how much attention they need from you.

Sectors are based on the movement of natural energy and help to block or channel the natural energy flow. While zones help to minimise the deployment of time and energy, there are no set boundaries around the zones. Zones flow from one to another without a specific border. There is no necessity to plant in concentric circles or other patterns, although often patterns are used, such as the Fibonacci spiral, which can increase the energy and aesthetics in your garden.

You start counting the zones from your own home "zone zero" and move from there outwards. Zone 1 is the area that can be found closest to your home and contains everything which needs a lot of attention and time. Herbs, salad vegetables, favourite flowers and new seedlings which need to be watered daily are good options for Zone 1. The further away the plants are from the house, the less likely it is that you will look after them properly. Raised beds, worm compost containers, greenhouses and animals which help you by eating scraps from the yard (such as rabbits, chickens, guinea pigs or ducks) are suitable for Zone 1.

The plants you put in Zone 2 also need a lot of attention, but not as much as those in Zone 1. Fruit trees, perennial vegetable plants, ponds, hedges, windbreaks, bee hives and bigger thermophilic compost systems are all suitable for Zone 2. All these need to be taken care of less often. Vegetables with longer ripening time and fewer harvests, such as potatoes, tubers, cauliflower and pumpkins are also good for Zone 2.

The next zones are normally found in larger plots, particularly in country areas. However, most urban backyards are capable of containing Zone 3 vegetation. Zone 3 contains plants which need little care. The only thing that they will probably need is mulch. These include large fruit and nut trees. On a farm it could be a large pasture.

Zone 4 is a semi-wild area which is used for wild-growing foods or wood production. In comparison, Zone 5 is a completely natural wilderness and nothing is farmed or cultivated on it. This area allows us to observe the natural cycles and patterns. Most Zone 5 areas are not to be found in urban regions.

While zoning helps you to organise your garden, you also need to know what to use and how often you need to harmonise the sectors of your garden to cope with the natural weather patterns and energy flows. Every area is pre-disposed to its own natural energy flow. This includes wind, sun, fire, water and even wild animals, all of which can significantly influence your landscape. There are various types of wind, such as hot summer winds, cold winds or salty winds, which often damage everything.

As soon as you become responsible for your sectors, you can implement certain design components which maximise or block the sector's natural energy. Using a clever design, you can prepare a sector for specific uses. The most important part of understanding sector dynamics in your environment is to observe carefully. Ideally, you should observe your land for one or two years before you begin with your design.

Failure to do so could result in your plants being subject to relentless sunshine or planting your tender vegetables within the territory of a clever food pilferer, or providing a rich food pantry for chickens or rabbits and not being able to protect your plants, no matter what you try to do. Fortunately, there are some modern aids to help you learn quickly how to use the power of the nature in your environment. People have gained knowledge over many years about the movement of the sun, the annual wind speeds and in which direction they blow.

There are plugins for Google Earth and Google Sketchup to determine the position of the sun and how to calculate the position of the shade on the ground, should you need it. Leafy trees provide excellent shade to protect from the summer sun. If you want to block the wind from certain areas, you can introduce plants which will provide protection from it. For example, conifers and huge sunflowers are splendid for protecting artichokes. Trees are excellent for providing a barrier against unwanted gazes. There are fire-resistant trees which can be planted in areas where there is a danger of fire. Most deciduous trees and bushes, for example, are fire-resistant.

CONCLUSION

Permaculture is a broad subject with many guiding principles, themes, philosophies and tools. However, everything can be summed up under the main aim of providing a durable, sustainable, functioning cycle in harmony with nature.

The most important of these philosophies have been explained and argued in order to give you a broad insight into the world of permaculture.

As you have read, all of us can do more to orientate ourselves in the direction of permaculture. It does not even mean restricting anything in our lifestyle. Particularly, when it has permeated through all social layers and is practised all over the world, it will lead to our world being a better place. If we live more against nature than in harmony with it, as we have been doing up to now, we will destroy everything which is necessary for survival within the foreseeable future.

Nature itself gives us the tools we need. We have only to recognise and use them. This knowledge is one of the central issues of permaculture. Even though the principles are so easy to understand, we find it so difficult to implement them.

Some ideas for practical implementation of permaculture are mentioned in this book. However, this is only a tiny taste of all the practical possibilities which are available to us. Because there are so many ways to start, there should be a tool for everyone to play a small part in improving the current situation.

Start today and lead the way. Use a little more permaculture to do your part in saving our planet!

DID YOU ENJOY MY BOOK?

Now you have read my book, you know to use permaculture to make the world a better place. This is why I am asking you now for a small favour. Customer reviews are an important part of every product offered by Amazon. It is the first thing that customers look at and, more often than not, is the main reason whether or not they decide to buy the product. Considering the endless number of products available at Amazon, this factor is becoming increasingly important.

If you liked my book, I would be more than grateful if you could leave your review by Amazon. How do you do that? Just click on the "Write a customer review"-button (as shown below), which you find on the Amazon product page of my book or your orders site:

Review this product

Share your thoughts with other customers

> Write a customer review

Please write a short note explaining what you liked most and what you found to be most important. It will not take longer than a few minutes, promise!

Be assured, I will read every review personally. It will help me a lot to improve my books and to tailor them to your wishes.

For this I say to you:

Thank you very much!

Yours

Lutz

DISCLAIMER

Printed in Great Britain
by Amazon